SALVATION IN SINGLENESS

Kyia's Keys

PREFIX

Many times singles feel as if there is no room for improvement in their spiritual lives in this state. Or as if God does not bless them as He does with those whom are married. Many times singles feel as though if they had a mate God would then give them the things that they so long desired. Neither statements are correct. Yes there is a blessing that comes with marriage but there is a form of sustenance that comes with being single. As you begin to sup with God more and learn the deepness of His heart while being single, when you obtain a mate you will then be able to teach your mate all that you know. When your marriage breaks forth into manifestation then the two of you will be stronger and bolder in your walk with the Lord. No matter what the world says about the ill-will of being single pay it no mind. Singleness is not God punishing you but God preparing you for whom He has for you. Remember in whom you marry that which you will become for the two shall become of one flesh joint together. Being married is a wonderful blessing but being single will allow an increase in ample time and space for you to be alone with the Lord. Marriage is a full time ministry and God has to equip you and give you the equipment to handle it. Honey hold your head up high and just know that there is a greater depth of salvation in your singleness and this short book will tell you all about it.

Enjoy!

As the gentle breeze flows through the air
As the waves in the water gently kiss the sea
As the birds hum their tune softly to a rhythm
As the kittens purr to show how much they love
As my hand softly touches your skin
As my lips press against yours
So is my love for you oh Lord forever more

~Salvation in Singleness~

Let's Get Down To It

One of the biggest problems many people face whether single or married is self infliction and self manipulation. You have to stop talking down to yourself and learn how to encourage yourself. The Bible tells us in ISamuel 30:6 (KJV) that David encouraged himself. If you have to look yourself in the mirror and say *"Hello beautiful"* then you do it. Tell yourself you are important, you are wonderful, you are vibrant etc… It all begins and ends with YOU! Satan plays within the mind of people because the mind is easily controlled. It retains information that sends the waves of information to the rest of the body. The mind holds the emotions, thoughts, and attitudes of an individual. The mind tells the body how to respond and react. If Satan can get into your mind than he can control the rest of your body and actions throwing you off the course that God wants you to take. Rebuke and bind anything that comes your way negatively and quicken yourself to praise God. Be it through singing or meditating on the word when negative thoughts arise in you. Leave no room in your mind or heart for anything negative to sit and fester. Once negativity is manifested within you it causes you to become a person whom you will not be pleased with. Henceforth, you cannot enter into the Kingdom of God with negativity dwelling in you such as unforgiveness. You must rid yourself of those things and move forward. Cleanse yourself of negative things and look towards the hills from whence cometh your help. Your help is already here the Lord has given it to you. Use it!

Part 1

As you are embarking on this journey just know that you are not alone and I am in this race with you. I am not the cheerleader on the sidelines yelling and screaming you can do it. No not at all honey. I am currently single and am waiting for God to move and manifest Himself greatly in this area of my life. It was and is not easy and I will expose that many nights I laid up asking God when my turn was to come. I cried, screamed, and hollered until my voice was raspy and sore to the Lord. I recall sitting up asking Him (the Lord) what is taking Him so long to deal with me in this area. I have witnessed ceremonies of my own friends, co-workers and even people I knew who were not walking in the statutes and principals of God. All the while sitting in the crowd I embraced and celebrated with them but still had that underlying feeling of the question: When? Whenever I would go to God in prayer even complaining to Him about being alone, He would respond by telling me to wait. Well my brothers and my sisters I will tell you that if you wait on the Lord and be of good courage you will endure to the very end. Not only will you endure but you will have the best mate you only read about in books and see in movies. When God's hand is in something it is in the best hands it can be in. Once I understood the Lord's concept and reasoning it became a little easier being alone (for I know it is just for a moment and season) and my strength in my singleness increased.

<u>Sidebar</u>

Do not find yourself worrying about friends, family, and colleagues whom are getting married before you. Just let them go first! Remember the Lord tells us in His word that the first shall be last and the last first Matthew 19:30 (KJV). Allow them to go ahead of you because when God finishes dealing with you, I am telling you my brothers and sisters not just your wedding, but your marriage will be greatly blessed! I decree it and declare it over you right now in the mighty name of Jesus Christ! Victory shall be your portion in your singleness. Never cease to keep praise on your lips. Never cease reading and meditating on the word of God. Never allow circumstances or situation to deteriorate you from the path that God has marked for you. I have your back in this segment of your life because I am going through it just the same. Cheer up because you have help and the best coach in the person of the Holy Spirit leading and guiding you into all manner of truth. I love you my brothers and sisters. You are doing a phenomenal job in your singleness. I am proud of you, God is proud of you, and Jesus is there with you holding out His hand. Take it and do not let go.

Part 2

In your singleness you are doing so much damage to the kingdom of hell then you can even think or imagine. Yes, I said it right! Through your singleness and faithfulness to the Lord the kingdom of darkness is trembling. Here is why. Not only are your prayers intensifying but your spiritual eyes are opening further, wider, and broader. The Apostle Paul says in ICorinthians 7:32 (KJV) *"But I would have you without carefulness. He that is unmarried careth for the things that belong to the Lord, how he may please the Lord:"*. As you continue your journey in singlehood you are strengthening your spirituality because you do not want to displease the Lord. Therefore, you are becoming more equipped in the spiritual realm and more aware in the natural. So, when God presents your mate to you, you will be able to recognize whom he or she is and be ready for marriage without a shadow of a doubt. This will eliminate choosing the wrong mate and ending up with someone that is not on your level whom cannot help meet your needs. When your spirituality is increased in the Lord you will not fall for anyone that comes your way and says: *"The Lord told me to tell you, you are my husband/wife"*. You will know within you that the individual standing in front of you is your mate. The Holy Ghost will begin to dance and jump within you so much that you cannot contain it. The Holy Ghost would almost scream at you and tell you that's the one. There he/she is!

Right about now your spiritual gifts within you are being birthed out of you that you had no comprehension of. For example, I have prayed to the Lord for the gift of intercession and totally forgotten that I prayed that specific prayer. As I was in the car one day with my sisters in Christ coming from a service the Spirit of the Lord pulled so heavy in me. I began to pray and almost immediately it intensified. Unbeknownst to me, the fire of God shot through me and the Holy Spirit was speaking through my lips in prayer. After it was all over (in which it was almost about an hour) my sister in Christ whom is an ordained minister looked at me and said: *"You have the gift of intercession"*. Maybe if I were married this gift would have taken time and space to manifest because marriage is not something you put on and off. You have to be submissive at all times for it is biblical. In my singleness my gifts, talents, and abilities are all being stirred and birthed out which is most likely the stage you are going through as well. Let the birthing process take place and just imagine how much spiritually equipped you will be when you become married.

Part 3

Understand your strength in serving the Lord with all your heart is being recognized and noticed. The recognition is not only by your peers but by those whom would never have had the courage to even say *"Hello"* to you. Your strength is not only predicated upon you, but it is for even myself, those around you, and those whom you do not know or recall. Your strength in your singleness breaks barriers in the spiritual realm like never before; as I mentioned about my gift of intercession. Now that I am able to go deep within my prayers along with warfare I can just imagine the spiritual havoc I am causing Hell. As you gain spiritual strength, when your mate comes, the two of you both joined together in prayer will be indestructible. You both will also become a total target and threat to Satan himself stronger. Yes, this will happen because Satan does not like unity or bondmanship. Receive it this way. If you think it is difficult now and you feel that the attacks of the enemy are heavy, just think how much more greater it will be when you come together with another individual. The Bible says in Matthew 18:20 *"For where two or three are gathered together in my name, there am I in the midst of them"*. When you and your spouse join together in prayer it increases a stirring in the spiritual realm and Satan begins to plot heavier. Satan will not like that you both prosper and be in good health as the word says according to IIIJohn 3. Therefore, continue to get equipped so you know what to pray against to cause it to be returned back to Hell. Pray and press on so your marriage will be all that you imagine.

I just want you to know and prepare you that marriage does come in seasons and cycles. Like the song says, you will have some good days and some hills to climb. This will happen if you both decide to have children, if the in-laws are living with you (which sometimes cause major hardships in marriages so think strategically about this one), you both are working long hours or one works in the morning and the other evenings, bills, and overall balancing your spirituality. These are the natural things that do occur, but you will get through it. Keep God at the center stage and keep prayer in the way and not out of the way. Just clearly grasp that when you are married everyday will not be milk and honey. Some days you will have water and butter (not in the literal sense). I want you to prepare yourself and know there will be rough days and all smiles another, but during those worse times you do not give up on each other. You both keep holding on to God's unchanging hand.

Part 4

Take your singleness as your pregnancy stage and your marriage the birthing place because then the fruit of your labor and travail is manifested; being naturally shown. There is a natural nine month process that mothers have to go through in order to have the baby come into this world healthy. If the baby comes before its time, then it is deemed premature. In many cases because the baby was not ready the child unfortunately passes away. However, the length in time God wants you to remain single just know that you are in labor with the Lord. As a mother eats for herself and the baby so it is with you and the Lord. He has to fill you with spiritual food and give you the knowledge that you need for yourself and your mate. When the baby is in this world and needs food, the mother gives the baby her milk that is stimulated from her breast, which is in the chest area close to the heart. Kyia what exactly are you saying? Well I am so very glad you asked! Once the Lord puts you and your mate together all that He (the Lord) has taught you and fed you with is easily transferred to your wife/husband. All that has been held up in your heart and soul will now be shared to your mate. This is the inner most depth parts of the heart that can only be accessible through the Lord revealing it. You and I both would never share our innermost deepest thoughts and heart with a person(s) we do not know or care much about. Some mother's will not breastfeed another women's child other than her own (naturally speaking). Enjoy the pregnancy! You will be even more blessed with the outcome of what you have birthed and delivered.

Although it would be wonderful and fantastic to have a mate, in this point in your walk with God you have to allow Him to finish working on you. Yes, you may feel lonely like you need another human being other than your walls to talk to, and you would like to have flesh hold and caress you at night. Just know God still needs to chisel some things off of you first. Remember those things are only temporal and are soon to come in due timing and season. Have I thought these thoughts? Yes! This is why I am able to freely write unto you. The Lord has and is bringing me through this trial so when my mate comes, I will be able to appreciate that which the Lord has blessed me with. Whenever that feeling of loneliness comes, ask the Lord to speak to your heart and to send the Angels to step into the room and comfort you. In this flesh dwells no good thing and it is deceitful, so it is important to overcome it and resist temptation. What your flesh may be yearning for now is only a temporary state. If you make a rational decision based on a temporary feeling you will pay an eternal consequence for your actions. Stay strong my brother and my sister for we all in this walk in God need you to survive.

<u>Sidebar</u>

If you have to hug that pillow real tight and cry, do so! There is no shame in it for many a nights I have gone through that phase, but the Lord allowed the Holy Spirit (the comforter) to comfort me in my time of grieving. I wrote: *"Weeping may only endure for a night, a moment, a time, and a season but joy has to come right afterwards"*. No matter how much crying you do at night or even during the day there is an overwhelming joy that has to soon follow. God will not leave you in that state for His word is true. Again, your strength is not just for you but for those whom look up to you, admire you, and those whom you have no knowledge of.

Part 5

In this stage and phase you are in, you have to develop the mentality that your spiritual walk with God is far more important than mortal man. Get the notion that you can depend on no one but God and not man. This will accelerate the marital process! If you pray that all you need is someone and not say to the Lord all you need is Him, He will not answer you. He is a jealous God and will have no other before Him. This includes your family, friends, loved ones, job, children, etc... My own mentality that I have developed is if the Lord sends me a husband fine if not, I am even better because I have Him. This I say and truly mean with all my heart because God is my provider and EVERYTHING! He brought me this far in my life and has me in the palm of His hand. People have treated and talked about me and to me any old kind of way. The Lord never did no such thing and will never do it to anyone. He is not man nor like unto man. He was by my side every step of the way even when I forsaken Him and did my own doings. When I came back to Him all He did was embrace me with open arms and never brought up what I had done. All He said to me was welcome back. You see men/women cannot be your everything for they did not create you nor did they know you before the foundation of the world. The Lord knew you which is why God has to be your everything. I know the songs say It, but you have to make up in your mind and heart that if God sends you someone, it is well and if He does not, it is still well.

Even though we are meant to be with someone (all in the timing and season of the Lord) there has to be a stable dependability on Him. I wrote in my previous book *Oh Husband Where Art Thou*? *"God's timing is never late"*. I reiterate these words because whenever we think that we are ready for something or the blessing that God wants to give us; we are actually not. If He gives us the blessing prematurely, we may end up destroying it and causing it to not last. For the number one prime example of why the divorce rate in the church is so high. The people involved probably did not wait to really hear from the Lord. They heard from their flesh within their thought process and in those two areas the Lord does not operate. He moves by His spirit and speaks to your heart. Not your mind. For this reason, many have divorced and have ruined good things. Wouldn't you want to wait for God to fully confirm whom it is you are to be with? Why jump into a relationship that could possibly destroy you spiritually, mentally, or emotionally? This is the primary purpose for this book. To give you encouragement in the waiting area and to enhance those things that God has already instilled in you. Trust and believe my brothers and sisters! This process will allow you to be a tremendous help to others who are single needing guidance and understanding.

Part 6

We all go through things in life to be of help to
others and not just ourselves. Your anointing and gifting
has nothing to do with you but it is for someone else. You
are not anointed to help yourself, but your anointing is for
you to help another. Notice how when you pray for
yourself it seems like almost years, months, and days go by
and nothing happens. Now when you pray for someone else
it seems as though God answered your prayer
expeditiously? This is because your anointing is not for you
just as your neighbors anointing is not for them. When
Jesus went into the garden to pray notice how the Lord did
not answer Him. I wonder what the outcome of the world
would have been if the Lord answered the prayers of the
disciples; had they gotten up to pray. I use this example to
show you that praying for yourself is a form of selfishness.
When you pray for your neighbor and your neighbor prays
for you, answers begin to take place and transform in the
Spiritual realm into the natural. If you are praying: *"Lord
bless me, bless my"* He will have nothing to do with that.
Once you being to say: *"Lord bless so and so, protect the
leaders, cover the church with the blood of Jesus, restore
marriages…etc"*; He will hear your call and answer your
declaration.

In your singleness, embrace the waiting room experience and while you are here, continue to keep praise upon your lips. Do not let go but hold on to the guardrail as you dance to the sweet melody of praise to our Father. Allow the Holy Spirit to whisper harmoniously to your heart that seeps into your soul. Let the fire of God burn within causing you to pant for Godly water that quenches the thirsty soul. Make room for Jesus as He steps in your surrounding area stretching forth His hand for a dance. As the train of the robe of the Father fills the room, grab hold of it and do not let go until He blesses you. Take your time and Waltz the dance floor of your prayer closet with the Lord. He longs to have you all to Himself with nothing on your mind and heart but Him. He is jealous for your attention. He wants to fill that empty void. He wants to fully equip you for marriage. He wants to be your bridegroom. He wants to be your all and all. He wants so much more than just a piece of your life. He wants it all! He longs to sit by your side as you mediate on the things of Him. While you are in the waiting room never cease to love Him. Never cease to give Him adoration. Never cease to give Him your heart. Lay your head to rest in His bosom as you pour out yourself to Him. Let Him stroke your head/hair and tell you He loves you. This is pure intimacy with the Lord. Flow in it.

Part 7

Allow God to keep working on your heart, your mind, and your emotions because they are very imperative when entering into a relationship. Only God knows the key and core details of what we need and want. Let Him give you the mate that you need as appose to the worlds formality of how your mate should physically look and respond to you. The world's concept and visuals are simply fairytales. There is no prince charming riding on a great big white horse to come and rescue you from the world, your problems, and in many cases; your family. There is no princess who scoops you up in her arms, kisses you, and your dreams of being all that you can be appear. No. Not so. Marriage is work which consists of praying, fasting, stability, security, respect etc… but most of all the trinity. God the Father, Jesus Christ, and God's Spirit (Holy Spirit/Ghost). Without these three entities being at the forefront of the marriage things are destined to fall apart and fail. Understand, true love and ecstasy comes within yourself and your mate when it is measured according to the word of God. How much Christ loves the church and the deepness of His heart is revealed throughout the chapters and verses. Read between the lines as you read the lines of this book. Whenever the mind is stimulated with melodious words that triggers thought, it then catapults it to vision that sends a wave message to the body to release itself to the individual. This is how we all have come into the body of Christ as one and developed such an intense relationship with Him. He gave us the messages through

His word and or through His servants in the vineyard. This triggered our physical nature to continue to go into the house (the building) to worship and praise.

<u>Sidebar</u>

Please also note that whatever pass hurt or pain you endured from your old relationship(s) they cannot and must not enter into the new. You cannot ask or make someone pay for the hurt and pain of another individual. This is why God has to finish chiseling the old man (person) off of you, so when he/she comes into your life you are fully whole and complete. I myself would be offended if a man came into my life and expected me to make up for all of the devastation, hurt, and pain he went through in pass relationships. Now if I would not like it done to me, I would not allow myself to do it to someone else. This is the mental development that you have to have within yourself. You must be emotionally ready for the new person who is coming so that no residue from the past can creep in tearing down which God has put together. Your past relationship(s) should have no dealings with the new. Finish getting over them by forgiving that person(s) whole heartedly and blessing them in prayer. A heart that forgives is a heart that will have freedom to worship God and love again. Had I not forgiven those people in my past, God would not have forgiven me. I John 4:20-21 (KJV) states: *"If a man say, I love God, and hateth his brother, he is a liar: for he that loveth not his brother whom he hath seen, how can he love God whom he hath not seen? And this commandment have we from him, That he who loveth God love his brother also"*.

Part 8

I will express if you feel that you cannot contain your physicality any longer and you need release in that area, pray to God to send your husband/wife expeditiously. The Apostle Paul states in ICorinthians 7:9 (KJV) *"But if they cannot contain, let them marry: for it is better to marry than to burn"*. You do not want to be condemned due to your flesh. There is a price and penalty to pay for each person you sleep with who is not your natural husband/wife. For whomever you lay down with they automatically become your spouse in the spiritual realm. This is due to the aspect of marriage being created and established in the beginning. Remember the Biblical principal and foundation of marriage according to Genesis 2:24; the two becoming of one flesh. Whomever you lay down with physically you become bound to them spiritually. For example, let's hypothetically say you never knew Christ and never knew His principals and lost your virginity while in high school at prom or in college. Years later you see that high school or college mate and something within you jumps. Later that same day, you find yourself having visions and/or dreams of them. That is because their spirit is indeed within you even after all of those years being passed on. When you are physical with someone, their spirit steps into your body and your spirit in them becoming intertwined. This is the spiritual aspect of the two becoming one.

My brothers and sisters in the Lord, I hope I have you thinking and considering yourself a bit more. I want the very best for you and your life. Settling for less than what you deserve for a moment of pleasure, is simply not worth it. The scripture tells us in Matthew 26:42 (KJV) *"watch and pray, that ye enter not into temptation: the spirit indeed is willing, but the flesh is weak"*. These were the words of our Lord and Savior Jesus Christ. He knew very well about temptation, as He was tempted on every side by the enemy. Yes Jesus was perfect in ALL His ways. But, as you see, He was still yet tempted and the greatest thing of all, was that he resisted. What would become of us if Jesus gave in to temptation? The Lord only knows where we would be.

Part 9

Well my brothers and my sisters I know you can manage and hang on to the Lord, because your wedding date is surely to come. Finish working on you and continue to lap in the luxury of the waiting room department. Sit and dine with the Angels and turn your dreams and goals into reality. Do not sulk at all but give God some praise. The song says to praise Him in advance. Tell the Lord thank you for your mate even right now whomever they are. Cover your mate right now in prayer saying wherever she/he is. Pray for your children whom you have not yet had on this earth. Pray for the businesses that are getting ready to open for they shall increase your giving to God and your community. Pray on a little while longer and watch the manifestation of your words come to pass. Decree and declare things over your life. Pray violently! The Bible says in Matthew 11:12 (KJV) *"And from the days of John the Baptist until now the kingdom of heaven suffereth violence, and the violent take it by force"*.

Sidebar

Brothers and sisters, it all starts and ends with you. Take care of you first so that you can obtain all and I mean ALL that God has for you. There is no greater joy then being fully prepared for the things that God has and wants to give us. He loves to see His children happy. When we are sad it makes Him sad. When He sees you and I, He sees an image of Himself. Grab hold of Him and squeeze Him tight. You will experience life like you never have before because of your obedience and righteousness unto the Lord. Do I have you smiling, thinking, understanding, or giggling? Salvation in singleness is amazing once you begin to enjoy it and all that you are as a human being. God is not punishing you. He is preparing you for the special gift of another soul to tend to. Once you understand and know how to take care of yourself spiritually and naturally, God will see fit to bless you in having a relationship. Notice how Adam in the garden had everything established before God presented Eve unto him. Adam was inwardly fulfilled in his duties within the garden, then God saw fit to bless him with Eve. Again, my brothers and sisters, it all starts and ends with YOU.

Final Thought

Be blessed and encouraged my brothers and sisters in the Lord. I am running this race with you. As you go about your day, remember to smile and thank God for the waiting room experience. This waiting time will not be for long. Ecclesiastes 9:11 (KJV) *"I returned, and saw under the sun, that the race is not to the swift, nor the battle to the strong..."*.

Amen

Purposeful Pain Ministries LLC is proud to announce the works of Kyia's Keys. Through her many hidden talents and abilities, she continues to be of help to all those in need. Kyia's wisdom, knowledge, and strength is very inspirational and encouraging. Come and embark on this journey of singleness while maintaining your salvation.

Purposeful Pain Ministries LLC
6650 Rivers Ave Suite 100
Charleston, SC 29406
purposefulpainmin@gmail.com
amazon.com/author/kyiaskeys